The Westminster Alice

A political parody based on
Lewis Carroll's Wonderland

by Hector Hugh Munro (Saki)

ILLUSTRATIONS BY
FRANCIS CARRUTHERS GOULD

WITH A FOREWORD BY
JOHN ALFRED SPENDER

AND AN AFTERWORD BY
HUGH CAHILL

evertype

2010

Published by Evertype, Cnoc Sceichín, Leac an Anfa, Cathair na Mart, Co. Mhaigh Eo, Éire. *www.evertype.com*.

First edition London: Westminster Gazette, 1902.

A catalogue record for this book is available from the British Library.

ISBN-10 1-904808-54-9
ISBN-13 978-1-904808-54-1

Typeset in De Vinne Text, Mona Lisa, ENGRAVERS' ROMAN, and *Liberty* by Michael Everson.

Illustrations: Francis Carruthers Gould, 1865.

Cover: Michael Everson.

"His Own Inventions" (text and cartoon) by kind permission of the University of Bristol Library, Special Collections.
"Afterword to the 2010 edition" by kind permission of King's College London, Foyle Special Collections Library.

Printed by LightningSource.

The Westminster Alice

Preface

Saki was the pen-name of Hector Hugh Munro (1870–1916). He was an author and playwright best known for his subtle and witty short stories. He wrote for periodicals such as the *Westminster Gazette*, the *Daily Express*, the *Bystander*, the *Morning Post*, and the *Outlook*.

Francis Carruthers Gould (1844–1925) was a political cartoonist and caricaturist who contributed to the *Pall Mall Gazette* until he joined the *Westminster Gazette* when it was founded. He later became an assistant editor for that publication. In addition to illustrating Saki's *Westminster Alice* in a series of publications from 1900 to 1902, Gould also illustrated Charles Geake's parody *John Bull's Adventures in the Fiscal Wonderland*, published in 1904.

The *Westminster Alice* vignettes were collected together and published in *Westminster Popular* No. 18 in 1902. Twenty-five years later, John Alfred Spender (1862–1942), who had edited the *Westminster Gazette* from 1896 until 1922, published them again with a foreword and a set of footnotes. These are re-published here, to help guide the reader into understanding and appreciating the context of Saki's parodies.

In his 1927 edition, Spender re-arranged the vignettes in chronological order—that is, in the order in which they had been published in the *Westminster Gazette*. Here, I have reverted to the order in which Saki had published them in 1902, as it seems to me that he may have arranged them thus for reasons of narrative or—well, to be honest, I don't know, but I'd rather not second-guess him. The dates of publication are given for those readers interested in the chronology, however.

The Ineptitude, White Queen, March Hare: Arthur Balfour (1848–1930), Member of Parliament for Manchester East, was First Lord of the Treasury and Leader of the House of Commons during Lord Salisbury's adminstration from 1895–1900.

Queen of Hearts, Red Queen, Mad Hatter: Joseph Chamberlain (1836–1914) was Secretary of State for the Colonies from 1895 to 1903. In 1899, with British public opinion supporting a war in support of the Uitlanders, he pressed for troop reinforcements which led to the Transvaal and the Orange Free State declaring war.

King of Hearts, Dormouse, Red King, Aged Man: Robert Cecil, 3rd Marquess of Salisbury (1830–1903) was Prime Minister from 1895 to 1902, serving also as Foreign Secretary during his tenure. He was uncle to Arthur Balfour. During his premiership was the Partition of Africa, which helped to precipitate the the Second Boer War.

The White Knight: Henry Petty-Fitz-maurice, 5th Marquess of Lansdowne (1845–1927). He was Governor-General of Canada 1883–1888, Viceroy of India 1888–1894, Secretary of State for War 1895–1900, and Foreign Secretary 1900–1905.

Duchess: Frederick Temple (1821–1902) was an English academic, teacher, and churchman, who served as Archbishop of Canterbury from 1896 until his death. Lambeth Palace is the official London residence of the Archbishop of Canterbury.

Cook: Samuel Smith (1836–1906) served as a Liberal MP for Liverpool from 1882 to 1885 and for Flintshire from 1886 to 1906. In 1909 the then Lord Mayor of Liverpool unveiled a memorial to Samuel Smith in honour of his life as a trader, politician and philanthropist. Hw was an outspoken critic of "ritualism" in the Church of England.

White King: Sir Henry Campbell-Bannerman (1836–1908) became leader of the Liberals in the House of Commons in 1898. The Boer War (1899–1902) had split the Liberal party into Imperialist and Pro-Boer camps and the party was defeated in the "khaki election" of 1900.

Unkhaki Messenger: John Morley, 1st Viscount Morley of Blackburn (1838–1923) was editor of the *Fortnightly Review* and of the *Pall Mall Gazette* before being elected MP for Newcastle upon Tyne. He opposed state intervention in social and economic matters

Primrose Courier, Second Flamingo, White Knight: Archibald Philip Primrose, 5th Earl of Rosebery (1847–1929) was Prime Minister from 1894 to 1895. He favoured the Boer War and opposed Home Rule for Ireland. His opposition to this latter policy meant that he could not participate in the Liberal Government of 1905.

First Flamingo, Five: Edward Grey, 1st Viscount Grey of Fallodon (1862–1933), better known as Sir Edward Grey, was Member of Parliament for for Berwick-upon-Tweed from 1885– 1916.

Caterpillar: William Court Gully, 1st Viscount Selby (1835–1909) was a British lawyer and Liberal politician who served as Speaker of the House of Commons between 1895 and 1905.

Humpty Dumpty: General Sir Redvers Henry Buller (1839–1908) was a British general and Victoria Cross holder. During the Second Boer War, he was defeated at the Battle of Colenso in December 1899, and broke the Seige of Ladysmith in February 1900.

White Rabbit: Alfred Austin (1835–1913) was an English poet, who was appointed Poet Laureate in 1896 upon the death of Alfred, Lord Tennyson. His poem "A Royal Home-Coming" is satirized by Saki in "Alice in a Fog".

Seven: Sir William Vernon Harcourt (1827–1904) was leader of the Liberal Party before Sir Henry Campbell-Bannerman. In 1898 he retired from the party, but as an independent in the years 1899–1900 he vigorously attacked the Conservative government's financial policy and attitude towards the Transvaal.

 *Two*: David Lloyd George, 1st Earl Lloyd-George of Dwyfor (1863–1945) was Member of Parliament for Caernarvon Boroughs. He was a vehement opponent of the Second Boer War and was strongly critical of Joseph Chamberlain.

In preparing this edition, I have in places modernized punctuation and capitalization to suit the preferences of the modern reader; Spender had made some of these changes in his 1927 edition, though the 1902 text has been used as the basis for the text here.

I am grateful to the University of Bristol Library, Special Collections, for permission to reproduce Francis Carruthers Gould's "His own Inventions", originally published in 1922, as an appendix to this edition.

I am likewise grateful to Hugh Cahill, Assistant Librarian at the Foyle Special Collections Library in King's College London for his permission to reprint, as an afterword, his 2008 review of *The Westminster Alice*, which first appeared on the web in a slightly different form as as one of continuing series of pieces based on notable items from the collections of the Foyle Special Collections Library.

Michael Everson
Westport 2010

Foreword to the 1927 edition

So far as the *Westminster Gazette* was concerned, "Saki" was the discovery of F. C. G. How they met, I don't know, but I have a clear recollection of Gould's bringing him to my room at the Office somewhere about the year 1900 and starting then and there on a discussion of articles which the one was to write and the other to illustrate. Saki left most of the talking to Gould, and at the beginning one had to dig hard to get a word out of him. But the word when it came was pungent and original, and in a few minutes I came to the conclusion that Gould was justified in his "find". The scheme suggested was that of *The Westminster Alice*—dealing with the South African War and politics in general—republished in this volume, and I own that I had misgivings about it. Parodies of the famous original had several times been submitted to me (as I suppose to most editors) and nearly all had been dismal failures. Such things must either succeed perfectly or fail lamentably, and to succeed perfectly meant not merely copying the form but catching the spirit of the inimitable fantastic original.

I cannot imagine anyone doubting that Saki is one of the few who have succeeded. Political parodies are generally dead within a few months of their first appearance, but *The Westminster Alice* is alive and sparkling after twenty-five years. In several of the sections it seems almost of no importance to recover the political allusions. The White Knight of "Alice in Pall Mall" remains the symbol of all the War-Ministers who never expected war, and it is a mere accident that he wears the face of the honoured veteran who happened to be in the saddle in 1899 when the unexpected came. His astonishing steed swathed in red-tape steps straight out of the old stable in Pall Mall with trappings devised by generations of Royal Dukes and plumed veterans. The Knight has the pensive melancholy broken by sudden happy thoughts that is so endearing in his prototype.

There is perhaps one touch which needs a little explanation. The reader who looks close will see hanging from the saddle a book labelled, *Bloch, is war impossible?* Emile Bloch, the Belgian strategical writer, had lately written an elaborate book in eleven volumes to prove that modern warfare on any large scale would be extraordinarily different from what most of the General Staffs supposed it would be, and W. T. Stead in his lively way had peptonized the eleven volumes into one and issued it with the title, *Is war impossible?* The appearance of "Alice in Pall Mall" with Stead's title in the cartoon moved M. Bloch to send me the whole eleven volumes to prove that he had said not that war was impossible, but something extremely different, and, as events proved, something extremely wise and prescient. I was glad that the correction came after and not before the publication of *The Westminster Alice*, for, if injustice was done to M. Bloch, by the same token an opening was given to Saki for one of his most brilliant strokes:

> "You see I had read a book written by some one to prove that warfare under modern conditions is impossible. You may imagine how disturbing that was to a man of my profession. Many men

would have thrown up the whole thing and gone home. But I grappled with the situation. You will never guess what I did."

Alice pondered. "You went to war, of course—"

"Yes, *but not under modern conditions.*"

The Knight stopped his horse so that he might enjoy the full effect of this announcement.

"Now, for instance," he continued kindly, seeing that Alice had not recovered her breath, "you observe this little short-range gun that I have hanging to my saddle? Why do you suppose that I have sent out guns of that particular kind? Because, if they happened to fall into the hands of the enemy, they'd be very little use to him. That was my own invention."

Of the many political squibs I can remember none had so immediate and complete a success as this. It was quoted everywhere, and the whole town joined in the laugh. The public at this time had long got over its "Mafficking" and was thoroughly annoyed at the mismanagement of the Boer War and its apparently interminable protraction in the guerilla stage. But the occasion was not so tragic as to forbid the play of this delicate raillery.

If "Alice in Pall Mall" explains itself, the same may be said of "Alice at Lambeth". Mr Samuel Smith, who is stirring the Protestant pot in Gould's picture, and Archbishop Temple who makes an inimitable Duchess, have indeed passed from the scene—passed, let us hope, to where Protestant and Anglo-Catholic are at rest—but there is the same trouble to-day in the Lambeth Kitchen as at the beginning of the century. Temple was one of Gould's favourites, and the benevolent Primate of these times is less tempting to the caricaturist, though scarcely less afflicted than his predecessor.

"Alice at St Stephen's" is in the same way perennial. It was addressed to Mr Gully and meant as a delicate rebuke of certain prim lawyer-like habits which had got on the nerves of the private member, but it will do for any Speaker from any member, and is a model of the subtle tactics which must be employed by critics of that illustrious functionary, if they do not wish to be haled to the bar of the House of Commons. The other sections are more topical, and though I have added a few notes to the text, something may be said here to explain the circumstances in which they were written.

The first section belongs to July 1900, and reflects the general uneasiness at the continuance of the Boer War after the taking of Pretoria. It had been a moot point since the war broke out whether the public was angrier with the Boers, the pro-Boers, or the Government, and, so far as the Government was concerned, much of the irritation fell upon Mr Arthur Balfour, the "Ineptitude" of Saki's satire. Herein, as I think the more intimate records will show, Mr Balfour suffered some wrong, but he had got labelled as the "philosophic doubter" and the phrase summed up all that the public found most irritating in the attitude of the Government, its air of being the victim of circumstances which no wisdom could have been expected to foresee, its apparently genuine surprise as the enemy proved to possess guns and to be well-mounted and extremely mobile and elusive. The Head of the Government, the illustrious Lord Salisbury, kept himself so entirely to himself during these months that it was easy to present him as fast asleep, and eventually as the somnolent dormouse of the Mad Hatter's tea-party. In the mean-time the formidable Red Queen (Mr Joseph Chamberlain) goes raging and tearing through the wood and her strident voice, demanding that every one shall wear khaki, sends a shiver down the spines of her more sedate and fastidious colleagues.

There follows the "khaki election" of 1900, and the Wonderland creatures, having triumphed over critics and satirists, are more complacent than ever. They are hard put to it to explain why the war, which they said was over with the taking of Pretoria, should still go on, but when Alice grows too inquisitive they fly to Christian Science or fall asleep. But Saki now gets a new opportunity with the Liberal Opposition, which all through 1900 and 1901 was in most evil plight between its retired leaders and its actual leaders, its "Lib. Imps" (Liberal Imperialists) and its pro-Boers. Campbell-Bannerman had not yet won the unique authority that he afterwards obtained, and in Saki's hands he is the bewildered White King vainly trying to record his emotions, while his followers go streaming after the Red King (Lord Rosebery) who after a long sleep in "rose coloured armour that had got a little rusty" had woke up with a crash in his famous Chesterfield speech (16 December 1901). The final picture carries back to the singular controversy which arose over the interpretation of that speech, the various gardeners (Sir William Harcourt, Sir Edward Grey, and Mr Lloyd George) each endeavouring to paint the rose in his own colour.

Saki was not of our political complexion, and, having had his fling at his own party, I rather think he enjoyed the opportunity of getting a little of his own back with these gentle gibes.

I cannot refrain from adding a word about Gould's part. Gould catches the spirit of Tenniel, though in his own rougher manner, with the same felicity as Saki does that of Lewis Carroll. I well remember the pleasure of both in this collaboration and their long consultations before the result was produced. Gould's frontispiece seems to me still a little masterpiece, and I hardly know where one could find concentrated in a small space so much of the character and flavour of the period dealt with in this satire.

J. A. Spender

Dedication to the 1902 Edition

With apologies to Sir John Tenniel and to everybody else concerned, including Messrs. Macmillan and Co., Limited, to whose courtesy we are indebted for permission to publish these political applications of the immortal adventures of Lewis Carroll's Alice.

The Westminster Alice

C O N T E N T S

"Alice", Child with dreaming eyes
  Noting things that come to pass
Turvey-wise in Wonderland
  Backwards through a Looking-Glass.

Figures flit across thy dream,
  Muddle through and flicker out
Some in cocksure blessedness,
  Some in Philosophic Doubt.

Some in brackets, some in sulks,
  Some with latchkeys on the ramp,
Living (in a sort of peace)
  In a Concentration Camp.

Party moves on either side,
  Checks and feints that don't deceive
Knights and Bishops, Pawns and all,
  In a game of Make-Believe.

Things that fall contrariwise,
  Difficult to understand
Darkly through a Looking-Glass
  Turvey-wise in Wonderland.

CHAPTER I[1]

Alice in Downing Street

"*H*ave you ever seen an Ineptitude?"[2] asked the Cheshire-Cat suddenly; the Cat was nothing if not abrupt.

"Not in real life," said Alice. "Have you any about here?"

"A few," answered the Cat comprehensively. "Over there, for instance," it added, contracting its pupils to the requisite focus, "is the most perfect specimen we have."

Alice followed the direction of its glance and noticed for the first time a figure sitting in a very uncomfortable attitude on nothing in particular. Alice had no time to wonder how it managed to do it; she was busy taking in the appearance of the creature, which was something like a badly-written note of interrogation and something like a guillemot, and seemed to have been trying to preen its rather untidy plumage with whitewash. "What a dreadful mess it's in!" she remarked,

---

1   First published in *Westminster Gazette*, 25 July 1900.
2   *The Ineptitude*: Mr A. J. (now Earl) Balfour, First Lord of the Treasury in Lord Salisbury's third Administration, 1895–1900.

after gazing at it for a few moments in silence. "What is it, and why is it here?"

"It hasn't any meaning," said the Cat, "it simply *is*."

"Can it talk?" asked Alice eagerly.

"It has never done anything else," chuckled the Cat.

"Can you tell me what you are doing here?" Alice inquired, politely. The Ineptitude shook its head with a deprecatory motion and commenced to drawl, "I haven't an idea."

"It never has, you know," interrupted the Cheshire-Cat rudely, "but in its leisure moments" (Alice thought it must have a good many of them) "when it isn't playing with a gutta-percha ball it unravels the groundwork of what people believe—or don't believe, I forget which."

"It really doesn't matter which," said the Ineptitude with languid interest.

"Of course it doesn't," the Cat went on cheerfully, "because the unravelling got so tangled that no one could follow it. Its theory is," he continued, seeing that Alice was waiting for more, "that you mustn't interfere with the inevitable. Slide and let slide, you know."

"But what do you keep it here for?" asked Alice.

"Oh, somehow you ca'n't help it; it's so perfectly harmless and amiable and says the nastiest things in the nicest manner, and the King just couldn't do without it. The King is only made of pasteboard, you know, with sharp edges; and the Queen—" here the Cat sank its voice to a whisper "—the Queen comes from another pack, made of Brummagem ware, without polish, but absolutely indestructible; always pushing, you know; but you ca'n't push an Ineptitude. Might as well try to hustle a glacier."

"That's why you keep so many of them about," said Alice.

"Of course. But its temper is not what it used to be. Lots of things have happened to worry it."

"What sort of things?"

"Oh, people have been dying off in round numbers, in the most ostentatious manner, and the Ineptitude dislikes fuss— but hush, here's the King coming."

His Majesty was looking doleful and grumpy, Alice thought, as though he had been disturbed in an afternoon nap. "Who is this, and what is that Cat doing here?" he asked, glancing gloomily at Alice and her companion.

"I really must ask you to give me notice of these questions," said the Ineptitude with a yawn.

"There's a dragon loose somewhere in the garden," the King went on peevishly, "and I am expected to help in getting it under control. Do I look as if I could control dragons?"

Alice thought he certainly did not.

"What do you propose doing?" drawled the Ineptitude.

"That's just it," said the King. "I say that whatever is done must be done cautiously and deliberately; the Treasurer says that whatever is done must be done cheaply—I am afraid the Treasurer is the weakest member of the pack," he added anxiously.

"Only made of Bristol board, you know," explained the Cat aside to Alice.

"What does the Queen say about it?" asked the Ineptitude.

with apologies to
Sir John Tenniel

"The Queen[3] says that if something is not done in less than no time there'll be a Dissolution."

Both looked very grave at this, and nothing was said for some minutes. The King was the first to break the silence. "What are you doing with that whitewash?" he demanded. "The Queen said everything was to be painted khaki."

---

3   *The Queen*: Mr Joseph Chamberlain, Secretary of State for the Colonies, 1895–1903.

"I know," said the creature pathetically, "but I had run out of khaki; the Unforeseen again, you know; and things needed whitewash so badly."

The Cat had been slowly vanishing during the last few minutes, till nothing remained of it but an eye. At the last remark it gave a wink at Alice and completed its eclipse.

When Alice turned round she found that both the King[4] and the Ineptitude were fast asleep.

"It's no good remaining here," she thought, and as she did not want to meet either the Queen or the dragon she turned to make her way out of the street.

"At any rate," she said to herself, "I know what an Ineptitude is like."

4 *The King*: The Marquess of Salisbury, Prime Minister, 1895–1902.

Alice in Pall Mall

"The great art in falling off a horse," said the White Knight,[6] "is to have another handy to fall on to."

"But wouldn't that be rather difficult to arrange?" asked Alice.

"Difficult, of course," replied the Knight, "but in my Department one has to be provided for emergencies. Now, for instance, have you ever conducted a war in South Africa?"

Alice shook her head.

"I have," said the Knight, with a gentle complacency in his voice.

"And did you bring it to a successful conclusion?" asked Alice.

"Not exactly to a *conclusion*—not a *definite* conclusion, you know—nor entirely successful either. In fact, I believe it's

---

5 First published in *Westminster Gazette*, 5 November 1900.

6a *The White Knight*: The Marquess of Lansdowne, Secretary of State for War, 1895–1900; became Foreign Secretary November, 1900, in succession to Lord Salisbury, who till then had been both Prime Minister and Foreign Secretary.

going on still.… But you ca'n't think how much forethought
it took to get it properly started. I dare say, now, you are
wondering at my equipment?"

Alice certainly was; the Knight was riding rather
uncomfortably on a sober-paced horse that was prevented
from moving any faster by an elaborate housing of red-tape
trappings. "Of course, I see the reason for that," thought
Alice. "If it were to move any quicker the Knight would come
off." But there were a number of obsolete weapons and
appliances hanging about the saddle that didn't seem of the
least practical use.

"You see, I had read a book," the Knight went on in a dreamy far-away tone, "written by someone to prove that warfare under modern conditions was impossible. You may imagine how disturbing that was to a man of my profession. Many men would have thrown up the whole thing and gone home. But I grappled with the situation. You will never guess what I did."

Alice pondered. "You went to war, of course—"

"Yes; *but not under modern conditions.*"

The Knight stopped his horse so that he might enjoy the full effect of this announcement.

"Now, for instance," he continued kindly, seeing that Alice had not recovered her breath, "you observe this little short-range gun that I have hanging to my saddle? Why do you suppose I sent out guns of that particular kind? Because if they happened to fall into the hands of the enemy they'd be very little use to him. That was my own invention."

"I see," said Alice gravely. "But supposing you wanted to use them against the enemy?"

The Knight looked worried. "I know there is that to be thought of, but I didn't choose to be putting dangerous weapons into the enemy's hands. And then, again, supposing the Basutos had risen, those would have been just the sort of guns to drive them off with. Of course they *didn't* rise; but they might have done so, you know."

At this moment the horse suddenly went on again, and the Knight clutched convulsively at its mane to prevent himself from coming off.

"That's the worst of horses," he remarked apologetically. "They are so Unforeseen in their movements. Now, if I had had my way I would have done without them as far as possible—in fact, I began that way, only it didn't answer. And yet," he went on in an aggrieved tone, "at Cressy it was the footmen who did the most damage."

"But," objected Alice, "if your men hadn't got horses how could they get about from place to place?"

"They couldn't. That would be the beauty of it," said the White Knight eagerly. "The fewer places your army moves to, the fewer maps you have to prepare. And we hadn't prepared very many. I'm not very strong at geography, but," he added, brightening, "you should hear me talk French."

"But," persisted Alice, "supposing the enemy went and attacked you at some other place—"

"They did," interrupted the Knight gloomily. "They appeared in strength at places that weren't even marked on the ordinary maps. But how do you think they got there?"

He paused and fixed his gentle eyes upon Alice as she walked beside him, and then continued in a hollow voice, "They rode. Rode and carried rifles. They were no mortal foes—they were Mounted Infantry."

6b The inscription on the mane of the Foreign Office horse is an allusion to Lord Lansdowne's reputed facility in the French language.

The Knight swayed about so with the violence of his emotion that it was inevitable that he should lose his seat, and Alice was relieved to notice that there was another horse with an empty saddle ready for him to scramble on to. There was a frightful dust, of course, but Alice saw him gathering the reins of his new mount into a bunch, and smiling down upon her with increased amiability.

"It's not an easy animal to manage," he called out to her, "but if I pat it and speak to it in French it will probably understand where I want it to go. And," he added hopefully, "it may go there. A knowledge of French and an amiable disposition will see one out of most things."

"Well," thought Alice as she watched him settling down uneasily into the saddle, "it ought not to take long to see him out of that."

CHAPTER III[7]

Alice at Lambeth

There was so much noise inside that Alice thought she might as well go in without knocking.

The atmosphere was as noticeable as the noise when Alice got in, and seemed to be heavily charged with pepper. There was a faint whiff of burning incense, and some candles that had just been put out were smouldering unpleasantly. Quite a number of Articles were strewn about on the floor, some of them more or less broken. The Duchess[8] was seated in the middle of the kitchen, holding, as well as she could, a very unmanageable baby that kept wriggling itself into all manner of postures and uncompromising attitudes. At the back of the kitchen a cook[9] was busily engaged in stirring up a large cauldron, pausing every now and then to fling a reredos or half a rubric at the Duchess, who maintained an air of placid unconcern in spite of the combined fractiousness of the baby and cook and the obtrusiveness of the pepper.

---

7 First published in *Westminster Gazette*, 12 December 1900.

8 *The Duchess*: Dr Temple, Archbishop of Canterbury.

9 *The Cook*: Mr Samuel Smith, M.P. for Liverpool, who was active in the Protestant cause.

"Your cook seems to have a very violent temper," said Alice, as soon as a lull in the discord enabled her to make herself heard.

"Drat her!" said the Duchess.

"I beg your pardon," said Alice, not quite sure whether she had heard aright. "Your Grace was remarking—"

"'Pax vobiscum', was what I said," answered the Duchess. "There's nothing like a dead language when you are dealing with a live volcano."

"But aren't you going to do something to set matters straight a bit?" asked Alice, dodging a whole set of Ornaments that went skimming through the air, and watching with some

18

anxiety the contortions of the baby, which was getting more difficult to hold every moment.

"Of course something must be done," said the Duchess,with decision, "but quietly and gradually—the leaden foot within the velvet shoe, you know."

Alice seemed to recognize the quotation, but she did not notice that anything particular was being done. "At the rate you're going, it will be years before you get settled," she remarked.

"Perhaps it will," said the Duchess resignedly. "I'm paid by the year, you know. *Festina lente*, say I."

"But surely you can keep some sort of order in your Establishment?" said Alice. "Why don't you exert your authority?"

"My dear, it takes me all the exertion I can spare to have any authority. I give orders, and it's my endeavour not to see that they're disobeyed. I'm sure I've given this child my Opinion—but there, you might as well opine to a limpet. As to the cook—"

Here the cook sent the pepper-pot straight at the Duchess, who broke of in a violent fit of sneezing. In the midst of the commotion the baby suddenly disappeared, and as the cook had taken up a new castor labelled "cayenne" Alice thought she might as well go and see where it had gone to. As she slipped out of the kitchen she heard the Duchess gasping between her sneezes, "Must—be done—quietly—and—gradually."

* * * *
* * *
* * * *

"What happened to the baby?" asked the Cheshire-Cat, appearing suddenly a few minutes later.

"It went out—to roam, I think," said Alice.

"I always said it would," said the Cat.

Alice and
the Liberal Party

Quite a number of them were going past, and the noise was considerable, but they were marching in sixes and sevens and didn't seem to be guided by any fixed word of command, so that the effect was not so imposing as it might have been. Some of them, Alice noticed, had the letters "I.L." embroidered on their tunics and headpieces and other conspicuous places ("I wonder," she thought, "if it's marked on their underclothing as well"); others simply had a big "L", and others again were branded with a little "e". They got dreadfully in each other's way, and were always falling over one another in little heaps, while many of the mounted ones did not seem at all sure of their seats. "They wo'n't go very far if they don't fall into better order," thought Alice, and she was glad to find herself the next minute in a spacious hall with a large marble staircase at one end of it. The White King[11] was

10 First published in *Westminster Gazette*, 30 November 1900.
11 *The White King*: Sir Henry Campbell-Bannerman.

sitting on one of the steps, looking rather anxious and just a little uncomfortable under his heavy crown, which needed a good deal of balancing to keep it in its place.

"Did you happen to meet any fighting men?" he asked Alice.

"A great many—two or three hundred, I should think."

"Not quite two hundred, all told," said the King, referring to his note-book.

"Told what?" asked Alice.

"Well, they haven't been told anything, exactly—yet. The fact is," the King Went on nervously, "we're rather in want of a messenger just now. I don't know how it is; there are two or three of them about, but lately they have always been either out of reach or else out of touch. You don't happen to have passed anyone coming from the direction of Berkeley Square?"[12] he asked eagerly.

Alice shook her head.

"There's the Primrose Courier,[13] for instance," the King continued reflectively, "the most reliable Messenger we have; he understands all about Open Doors and Linked Hands and all that sort of thing, and he's quite as useful at home. But he frightens some of them nearly out of their wits by his Imperial Anglo-Saxon attitudes. I wouldn't mind his skipping about so if he'd only come back when he's wanted."

"And haven't you got anyone else to carry your messages?" asked Alice sympathetically.

"There's the Unkhaki Messenger,"[14] said the King, consulting his pocket-book.

---

12 Berkeley Square, Lord Rosebery's residence (No. 38).

13 *The Primrose Courier*: Lord Rosebery, leader of the Liberal Imperialists.

14 *The Unkhaki Messenger*: Mr John (afterwards Viscount) Morley, who had been active as an anti-Imperialist. Mr Morley had recently produced his book on Oliver Cromwell, and Lord Rosebery his book on Napoleon at St Helena, entitled *Napoleon: The Last Phase*. Lord Rosebery had resigned the leadership of the Liberal Party in 1896,

"I beg your pardon," said Alice.

"You know what Khaki means, I suppose?"

"It's a sort of colour," said Alice promptly. "Something like dust."

"Exactly," said the King; "Thou dost—he doesn't. That's why he's called the Unkhaki Messenger."

Alice gave it up.

"Such a dear, obliging creature," the King went on, "but so dreadfully unpunctual. He's always half a century in front of his times or half a century behind them, and that puts one out so."

Alice agreed that it would make a difference.

and Mr Morley had retired from the "councils of the party" in 1898. But both had reappeared on the scene and the allusions are to Sir Henry Campbell-Bannerman's perplexities at their disappearances and reappearances.

"It's helped to put us out quite six years already," the King went on plaintively, "but you ca'n't cure him of it. You see, he will wander about in byways and deserts, hunting for Lost Causes, and whenever he comes across a stream, he always wades against the current. All that takes him out of his way, you know; he's somewhere up in the Grampian Hills by this time."

"I see," said Alice. "That's what you mean by 'being out of touch'. And the other Messenger is—"

"Out of reach," said the King. "Precisely."

"Then it follows—" said Alice.

"I don't know what you mean by 'it'," interrupted the King, sulkily. "No one follows. That is why we stick in the same place. DON'T!" he suddenly screamed, jumping up and down in his agitation. "Don't do it, I say."

"Do what?" asked Alice in some alarm.

"Give advice. I know you're going to. They've all been doing it for the last six weeks. I assure you the letters I get—"

"I wasn't going to give you advice," said Alice indignantly, "and as to letters, you've got too much alphabet as it is."

"Why, you're doing it now," said the King angrily. "Goodbye."

As Alice took the hint and walked away towards the door she heard him calling after her in a kinder tone: "If you *should* meet anyone coming from the direction of Berkeley Square—"

CHAPTER V[15]

Alice Anywhere but in Downing Street

"I don't know what business you have here," the Red Queen[16] was saying, "If you don't belong to the Cabinet. Of course," she added more kindly, "you maybe one of the outer ring. There are so many of them, and they're mostly so unimportant, that one ca'n't be expected to remember *all* their faces."

"What is *your* business?" asked Alice, by way of evading the question.

"There isn't any business really," said the White Queen.[17] "Her Red Majesty sometimes says more than she means. Fancy," she added eagerly, "I went round in 85 yesterday!"

"Round what?" asked Alice.

"The Links, of course."

---

15 First published in *Westminster Gazette*, 11 October 1901.
16 *The Red Queen*: Mr Joseph Chamberlain.
17 *The White Queen*: Mr Balfour, whose favourite occupation was supposed to be golf.

"Talking about a Lynx," said the Red Queen, "are you any good at Natural History? Take prestige from a Lion, what would remain?"

"The prestige wouldn't, of course," said Alice, "and the Lion might not care to be without it. I suppose nothing—"

"*I* should remain, Whatever happened," said the Red Queen with decision.

"She's no good at Natural History," observed the White Queen. "Shall I try her with Christian Science? If there was a sort of warfare going on in a kind of a country, and you wanted to stop it, and didn't know how to, what course of inaction would you pursue?"

"Action, you mean. Her White Majesty occasionally muddles things," interposed the Red Queen.

"It amounts to much the same thing with us," said the White Queen.

Alice pondered. "I suppose I should resign," she hazarded.

Both Queens gasped and held up their hands in reprobation.

"A most improper suggestion," said the White Queen severely. "Now I should simply convince my reasoning faculty that the war didn't exist—and there'd be an end of it."

"But," objected Alice, "supposing the war was to assume that your reasoning faculty was wanting, and went on all the same?"

"The child is talking nonsense," said the Red Queen. "She doesn't know anything of Christian Science. Let's try Political Economy. Supposing you were pledged to introduce a scheme for Old Age Pensions,[18] what would be your next step?"

Alice considered. "I should think—"

"Of course you'd think," said the White Queen. "Ever so much. You'd go on thinking off and on for years. I ca'n't tell

---

18 Old Age Pensions: Mr Chamberlain had pledged himself to a scheme of Old Age Pensions, and he was much criticized by the Opposition in these years for postponing or evading the fulfilment of this pledge.

you how much I've thought about it myself; I still think about it a little, just for practice—principally on Tuesdays."

"I should think," continued Alice, without noticing the interruption, "that the first thing would be to find the money."

"Dear, no," said the Red Queen pityingly, "*that* wouldn't be Political Economy. The first thing would be to find an excuse for dropping the question."

"What a dreadful lot of unnecessary business we're talking!" said the White Queen fretfully. "It makes me quite miserable—carries me back to the days when I was in Opposition. Ca'n't she sing us something?"

"What shall I sing you?" asked Alice.

"Oh, anything soothing; the '*Intercessional*', if you like."

Alice began, but the words didn't come a bit right, and she wasn't at all sure how the Queens would take it:—

Voice of the People, lately polled,
    Awed by our broad-cast battle scheme,
By virtue of whose vote we hold
    Our licence still to doze and dream,
Still, falt'ring Voice, complaisant shout,
    Lest we go out, lest we go out.

Alice looked anxiously at the Queens when she had finished, but they were both fast asleep.

"It will take a deal of shouting to rouse them," she thought.

CHAPTER VI[19]

Alice in Difficulties

"How are you getting on?" asked the Cheshire-Cat.
"I'm not," said Alice.
Which was certainly the truth.

19 First published in *Westminster Gazette*, 9 October 1901. The
"difficulties" are those of the Liberal Party in 1901. The first

It was the most provoking and bewildering game of croquet she had ever played in. The other side did not seem to know what they were expected to do, and, for the most part, they weren't doing anything, so Alice thought she might have a good chance of winning—though she was ever so many hoops behind. But the ground she had to play over was all lumps and furrows,[20] and some of the hoops were three-cornered in shape, which made them difficult to get through, while as for the balls (which were live hedgehogs[21] and very opinionated), it was all she could do to keep them in position for a minute at a time. Then the flamingo which she was using as a mallet kept stiffening itself into uncompromising attitudes, and had to be coaxed back into a good temper.

"I think I can manage *him* now," she said. "Since I let him have a latchkey and allowed him to take up the position he wanted, he has been quite amiable. The other flamingo I was playing with," she added regretfully, "strayed off into a furrow. The last I saw of it, it was trying to bore a tunnel."

"A tunnel?" said the Cat.

"Yes; under the sea, you know."

"I see; to avoid the cross-current, of course."

---

flamingo (p. 29) is Sir Edward Grey, the second (p. 31) Lord Rosebery.

20 The "furrow" is an allusion to a speech in which Lord Rosebery had said, "I must plough my furrow alone" (July 1901). "Cross-currents" was the term usually employed for differences in the Liberal Party.

21 One of the hedgehogs (p. 29) is labelled "Rattigan", and the other "I.L.P." (Independent Labour Party) on one side and "L.I." (Liberal Imperialist) on the other. This is an allusion to the North-East Lanark by-election in September 1901, when Sir W. H. Rattigan secured the seat through a split in the Liberal and Radical vote, Mr Cecil Harmsworth standing as a Liberal Imperialist and Mr R. Smillie as an Independent Labour candidate.

Alice waited till the Cat had stopped grinning at its own joke, and then went on:—

"As for the hedgehogs, there's no doing anything with them; they've got such prickly tempers. And they're *so* short-sighted; if they don't happen to be looking the same way they invariably run against each other. I should have won that last hoop if both hedgehogs hadn't tried to get through at the same time!"

"Both?"

"Yes, the one I *was* playing with and the one I wasn't. And everyone began shouting out all sorts of different directions till I scarcely knew which I *was* playing with. Really," she continued plaintively, "it's the most discouraging croquet-party I was ever at; if we go on like this there soon wo'n't be any party at all."

"It's no use swearing and humping your back," said the Cat sympathetically." (Alice hadn't done either.) "Keep your temper and your flamingo."

"Is that all?"

"No," said the Cat; "keep on playing *with the right ball*."

"Which *is* the right ball?" asked Alice.

But the Cat had discreetly vanished.

Alice at St Stephen's

"It's very provoking," said Alice to herself; she had been trying for the previous quarter of an hour to attract the attention of a large and very solemn caterpillar that was perched on the top of big mushroom with a Gothic fringe. "I've heard that the only chance of speaking to it is to catch its eye," she continued, but she found out that however perseveringly she thrust herself into the Caterpillar's[23] range of vision its eye persistently looked beyond her, or beneath her, or around her—never at her. Alice had read somewhere that little girls should be seen and not heard. "But," she thought, "I'm not even seen here, and if I'm not to be heard, what am I here at all for?" In any case she determined to make an attempt at conversation.

"If you please—" she began.

"I don't," said the Caterpillar shortly, without seeming to take any further notice of her.

After an uncomfortable pause she commenced again.

---

22 First published in *Westminster Gazette*, 11 June 1901.
23 *The Caterpillar*: Mr Speaker Gully.

"I should like—"

"You shouldn't," said the Caterpillar with decision.

Alice felt discouraged, but it was no use to be shut up in this way, so she started again as amiably as she could.

"You ca'n't think, Mr Caterpillar—"

"I can, and I often do," he remarked stiffly; adding, "You mustn't make such wild statements. They're not relevant to the discussion."

"But I only said that in order—"

"You didn't," said the Caterpillar angrily. "I tell you it was not in order."

"You are so dreadfully short," exclaimed Alice; the Caterpillar drew itself up.

"In manner, I mean; no—in memory," she added hastily, for it was thoroughly angry by this time.

"I'm sure I didn't mean anything," she continued humbly, for she felt that it was absurd to quarrel with a caterpillar.

The Caterpillar snorted.

"What's the good of talking if you don't mean anything? If you've talked all this time without meaning anything you're not worth listening to."

"But you put a wrong construction—" Alice began.

"You ca'n't discuss Construction now, you know; that comes on the Estimates. Shrivel!"

"I don't understand," said Alice.

"Shrivel. Dry up," explained the Caterpillar, and proceeded to look in another direction, as if it had forgotten her existence.

"Good-bye," said Alice, after waiting a moment; she half hoped that the Caterpillar might say "See you later," but it took not the slightest notice of her remark, so she got up reluctantly and walked away.

"Well, of all the gubernatorial—" said Alice to herself when she got outside. She did not quite know what it meant, but it was an immense relief to be able to come out with a word of six syllables.

CHAPTER VIII[24]

Alice Lunches at Westminster

"*I* think I would rather not hear it just now," said Alice, politely.

"It is expressly intended for publication," said Humpty Dumpty.[25] "I don't suppose there'll be a paper to-morrow that wo'n't be talking about it."

"In that case I suppose I may as well hear it," said Alice with resignation.

"The scene," said Humpty Dumpty, "is Before Ladysmith, and the time—well, the time is After Colenso:—

---

24 First published in *Westminster Gazette*, 14 October 1901.

25 *Humpty Dumpty*: General Sir Redvers Buller, V.C. On his return from South Africa in 1901, Sir Redvers was appointed to command the first Army Corps at Aldershot in pursuance of a new Army Reorganization Scheme. There was much criticism of the appointment and on 10 October he answered his critics in a singular speech at the Queen's Hall, Westminster, in which he specially defended himself against the charge that he had counselled the surrender of Ladysmith. His defence was that in heliographing instructions to Sir George White, when he was locked up in Ladysmith, he had

I sent a message to the White
To tell him—if you MUST, you might;
But then, I said, you p'raps might
  not
(The weather was EXTREMELY hot).
This query, too, I spatchcock-slid,
How would you do it, if you did?
I did not know, I rather thought—
And then I wondered if I ought."

"spatchcocked" a passage which would have relieved Sir George of responsibility in case he had found it necessary to surrender, and that this passage had been ungenerously twisted into an instruction to surrender. The speech was so confused and eccentric that it greatly perplexed the public, and ten days later the Government cancelled his appointment on the ground that he had committed a breach of regulations in making it. Sir Redvers suggested in his speech that the Boers had put dead horses into the river Tugela, in order to poison the water for the besieged garrison.

"It's dreadfully hard to understand," said Alice.

"It gets easier as it goes on," said Humpty Dumpty, and resumed.

"They tried a most malignant scheme,
They put dead horses in the stream;
(With One at home I saw it bore
On preference for a horseless war).
But though I held the war might cease,
At least I never held my peace.
I held the key; it was a bore
I could not hit upon the door.
Then One suggested, in my ear,
It would be well to persevere.
The papers followed in that strain,
THEY said it very loud and plain.
I simply answered with a grin,
'Why, what a hurry they are in.'
I went and played a waiting game;
Observe, I got there just the same.
And if you HAVE a better man,
Well, show him to me, IF you can."

"Thank you very much," said Alice. "It's very interesting, but I'm afraid it wo'n't help to cool the atmosphere much."

"I could tell you lots more like that," Humpty Dumpty began, but Alice hastily interrupted him.

"I hear a lot of fighting going on in the wood; don't you think I had better hear the rest some other time?"

Alice in a Fog

"The Duke and Duchess!"[27] said the White Rabbit nervously as it went scurrying past. "They may be here at any moment, and I haven't got it yet."

"Hasn't got what?" wondered Alice.

"A rhyme for Cornwall," said the Rabbit, as if in answer to her thought. "Borne well, yawn well—" and he pattered away into the distance, dropping in his hurry a folded paper that he had been carrying.

---

26 First published in *Westminster Gazette*, 11 November 1901.

27 The Duke of York (now King George V) visited Australia accompanied by the Duchess to open the first session of the Australian Commonwealth Parliament on 7 May 1901, and the Poet

"What have you got there?" asked the Cheshire-Cat as Alice picked up the paper and opened it.

"It seems to be a kind of poetry," said Alice doubtfully. "At least," she added, "some of the words rhyme and none of them appear to have any particular meaning."

"What is it about?" asked the Cat.

"Well, someone seems to be coming somewhere from everywhere else and to get a mixed reception:—

> *... Your Father smiles,*
> *Your Mother weeps.*"

"I've heard something like that before," said the Cat. "It went on, if I remember, 'Your aunt has the pen of the gardener'."

"There's nothing about that here," said Alice. "Supposing she didn't weep when the time came?"

"She would if she had to read all that stuff," said the Cat. "And then it goes on:—

> *You went as came the swallow.*"

"That doesn't help us unless we know how the swallow came," observed the Cat. "If he went as the swallow usually travels he would have won the Deutsch Prize."[28]

> "*... homeward draw*
> *Now it hath winged its way to winters green.*

Laureate (Mr Alfred Austin) improved the occasion by writing a royal and loyal ode to greet him on his return. Mr Austin's poems had been frequently the subject of Gould's satire, and Saki takes up the theme.

28 A prize given for aviation in its early days.

"There seems to have been some urgent reason for avoiding the swallow," continued Alice. "Then all sorts of things happened to the Almanac:—

Twice a hundred dawns, a hundred noons, a hundred eves.

"You see there were two dawns to every noon and evening—it must have been dreadfully confusing."
"It would be at first, of course," agreed the Cat.
"I think it must have been that extra dawn that

Never swallow or wandering sea-bird saw,

or else it was the Flag."

"What flag?"
"Well, the flag that someone found,

Scouring the field or furrowing the sea."

"Would you mind explaining," said the Cat, "which was doing the scouring and furrowing?"

"The Flag," said Alice, "or the someone. It isn't exactly clear, and it doesn't make sense either way, Anyhow, wherever the Flag was unfurled it floated o'er the Free."
"Come, that tells us something. Whoever it was must have avoided Dartmoor and St Helena."

"*You, wandering, saw,*
Young Commonwealths you found."

"There's a great deal of wandering in the poem," observed the Cat.

"*You sailed from us to them, from them to us,*" continued Alice.

"That isn't new, either. It *should* go on: '*You all returned from him to them, though they were mine before*'."

"It doesn't go on quite like that," said Alice. "It ends up with a lot of words that I suppose were left over and couldn't be fitted in anywhere else:

> *Therefore rejoicing mightier hath been made*
> *Imperial power.*"

"That," said the Cat, "is the cleverest thing in the whole poem. People see that at the end, and then they read it through to see what on earth it's about."

"I'd give sixpence to anyone who can explain it," said Alice.

Alice has Tea at the Hotel Cecil[30]

*T*he March Hare and the Dormouse and the Hatter were seated at a very neglected-looking tea-table; they were evidently in agonized consideration of something—even the Dormouse, which was asleep, had a note of interrogation in its tail.

"No room!" they shouted, as soon as they caught sight of Alice.

"There's lots of room for improvement," said Alice, as she sat down.

"You've got no business to be here," said the March Hare.

---

29 First published in *Westminster Gazette*, 29 November 1901.

30 Lord Salisbury's Government was frequently spoken of in popular jest as the "Hotel Cecil" in allusion to the supposed predominance of the Cecil family in its composition. The *March Hare* is Mr Balfour, the *Mad Hatter* is Mr Chamberlain, and the *Dormouse* is Lord Salisbury. The Boer War, supposed to have been over in September 1900, is still going on, and the Irish question has again begun to trouble the Government.

"And if you had any business you wouldn't be here, you know," said the Hatter. "I hope you don't suppose this is a business gathering. What will you have to eat?" he continued.

Alice looked at a long list of dishes with promising names, but nearly all of them seemed to be crossed off.

"That list was made nearly seven years ago, you know," said the March Hare, in explanation.

"But you can always have patience," said the Hatter. "You begin with patience and we do the rest." And he leaned back and seemed prepared to do a lot of rest.

"Your manners want mending," said the March Hare suddenly to Alice.

"They don't," she replied indignantly.

"It's very rude to contradict," said the Hatter. "You would like to hear me sing something."

Alice felt that it would be unwise to contradict again, so she said nothing, and the Hatter began:

Dwindle, dwindle, little war,
How I wonder more and more,
As about the veldt you hop
When you really mean to stop.

"Talking about stopping," interrupted the March Hare anxiously, "I wonder how my timepiece is behaving."

He took out of his pocket a large chronometer of complicated workmanship, and mournfully regarded it.

"It's dreadfully behind the times," he said, giving it an experimental shake. "I would take it to pieces at once if I was at all sure of getting the bits back in their right places."

"What is the matter with it?" asked Alice.

"The wheels seem to get stuck," said the March Hare. "There is too much Irish butter in the works."

"Ruins the thing from a dramatic point of view," said the Hatter. "Too many scenes, too few acts."

"The result is we never have time to get through the day's work. It's never even time for a free breakfast-table; we do what we can for education at odd moments, but we shall all die of old age before we have a moment to spare for social duties."

"You might lose a lot if you run your business in that way," said Alice.

"Not in this country," said the March Hare. "You see, we have a Commission on everything that we don't do."

"The Dormouse must tell us a story," said the Hatter, giving it a sharp pinch.

The Dormouse awoke with a start, and began as though it had been awake all the time: "There was an old woman who lived in a shoe—"

"I know," said Alice, "she had so many children that she didn't know what to do."

"Nothing of the sort," said the Dormouse. "You lack the gift of imagination. She put most of them into Treasuries and Foreign Offices and Boards of Trade, and all sorts of unlikely places where they could learn things."

"What did they learn?" asked Alice.

"Painting in glowing colours, and attrition, and terminology (that's the science of knowing when things are over), and iteration (that's the same thing over again), and drawing—"

"What did they draw?"

"Salaries. And then there were classes for foreign languages. And such language!" (Here the March Hare and the Hatter shut their eyes and took a big gulp from their tea-cups.) "However, I don't think anybody attended to them."

The Dormouse broke off into a chuckle which ended in a snore, and as no one seemed inclined to wake it up again, Alice thought she might as well be going.

When she looked back the Hatter and the March Hare were trying to stiffen the Dormouse out into the attitude of a lion guardant. "But it will never pass for anything but a Dormouse if it will snore so," she remarked to herself.

Alice goes to Chesterfield [32]

*A*lice noticed a good deal of excitement going on among the Looking-glass creatures: some of them were hurrying off expectantly in one direction, as fast as their legs would carry them, while others were trying to look as if nothing in particular was about to happen.

"Those mimsy-looking birds," she said, catching sight of a group that did not look in the best of spirits, "those must be

31 First published in *Westminster Gazette*, 16 December 1901.
32 Lord Rosebery's speech at Chesterfield on 16 December was the chief event in Liberal politics in the winter of 1901. It caused extraordinary interest and commotion both before and after, and though the South African parts of it were hailed equally by both sections of the party, it opened a new line of division in domestic policy, to the great embarrassment of Sir Henry Campbell-Bannerman (*The White King*). The picture "Spades in Wonderland" (p. 56) represents the efforts of the different party gardeners, Sir William Harcourt, Sir Edward Grey, and Mr Lloyd George, to paint the rose their own colour, i.e. to make the speech mean what they wished it to mean.

Borogoves. I've read about them somewhere; in some parts of the country they have to be protected. And, I declare, there is the White King coming through the wood."

after Tenniel

Alice went to meet the King, who was struggling with a very unwieldy pencil to write something in a notebook. "It's a memorandum of my feelings, in case I forget them," he explained. "Only," he added, "I'm not quite sure that I meant to put it that way."

Alice peeped over his shoulder and read: "The High Commissioner may tumble off his post; he balances very badly."

"Could you tell me," she asked, "what all the excitement is about just now?"

"Haven't an idea," said the White King, "unless it's the awakening."

"The what?" said Alice.

"The Red King, you know; he's been asleep for ever so long, and he's going to wake up to-day. Not that it makes any difference that I can see—he talks just as loud when he's asleep."

Alice remembered having seen the Red King, in rose-coloured armour that had got a little rusty, sleeping uneasily in the thickest part of the wood.

"The fact is," the White King went on, "some of them think we're only a part of his dream, and that we shall all go 'piff' when he wakes up. That is what makes them so jumpy just now. Oh!" he cried, giving a little jump himself. "There go some more!"

"What are they?"' asked Alice, as several strange creatures hurtled past, like puff-balls in a gale.

"'They're the Slithy Toves," said the King, "Libimps and Jubjubs and Bandersnatches. They're always gyring and gimbling wherever they can find a wabe."

"Where are they all going in such a hurry?" Alice asked.

"They're going to the meeting to hear the Red King," the White King said in rather a dismal tone. "They've all got latchkeys," he went on, "but they'd better not stay out too late."

Here the White King gave another jump. "What's the matter?" asked Alice.

"Why, I've just remembered that I've got a latchkey too, my very own! I must go and find it." And away went the White King into the wood.

"How these kings do run about!" thought Alice. "It seems to be one of the Rules of the Game that when one moves the other moves also."

The next moment there was a deafening outburst of drums, and Alice saw the Red King rushing through the wood with a big roll of paper.

"Dear me!" she heard him say to himself as he passed. "I hope I sha'n't be late for the meeting, and I wonder how they'll take my speech."

Alice noticed that the Borogoves made no attempt to follow, but tried to look as if they didn't care a bit. And away in the distance she heard a sort of derisive booing, with a brogue in it. "That must be the Mome Raths outgribing," she thought.

T H E   A G E D   M A N[33]

33 First published in *Westminster Gazette*, 16 May 1901.

I shook him well from side to side
Until his face was blue.
"Come, tell me where's the Bill," I cried,
"And what you're going to do."
He said, "I hunt for gibes and pins
To prick the Bishops' calves,
I search for Royal Commissions, too,
To use as safety valves."

[See the Debate on Temperance Legislation
in the House of Lords, 14 May 1901][34]

---

34 Lord Salisbury chaffed the Bishops and suggested another Royal
Commission as the next step, thereby evoking a spirited reply from
Lord Rosebery.

THE RED KING: Harcourt, Grey, and Lloyd-George are all putting their own colours on; I think I'd better paint it myself.

---

35 First published in *Westminster Gazette*, 24 January 1902. See footnote 32, p. 49 above.

His Own Inventions

H i s   O w n   I n v e n t i o n s [36]

A n   i l l u s t r a t e d   A l i c e   s t o r y
b y   F r a n c i s   C a r r u t h e r s   G o u l d

*A*lice heard the steps of a horse moving through the wood, and presently a Knight rode out into the open glade. He was dressed in tin armour and had rather long white hair. He sat very stiffly, standing up in his stirrups and keeping tight hold of the reins, for he did not seem to be on the best of terms with his horse.

But what attracted Alice's attention most was the strange assortment of articles which belonged to the horse and the rider. There was a gibbet, and a large sack which seemed to be empty, a huge extinguisher, a sieve, what looked like a big doll's house, a beehive, a bag of golf clubs, and a wooden box, like a collecting-box, only the bottom lid was hanging open.

Alice looked at this collection with great curiosity.

"I see youre admiring my little contrivances," the Knight said in a friendly tone. "They're all my own invention!"

Alice came a little closer to examine them. "But what is that?" she asked, pointing to the gibbet.

---

36 First published in *Westminster Gazette*, 7 February 1922.

The Knight leaned towards her, and in a confidential whisper said: "Don't mention it again—but it's to hang the Kaiser on. I said I would, and so, of course, I had to prepare for it. You see, all I had to do was catch the Kaiser, put his head in the noose, and there you were, or rather he would have been!"

"But you didn't hang him, did you?" said Alice. "I never heard of it."

"No, not exactly," the Knight replied, a shade of vexation passing over his face. "He didn't come to be hanged; indeed, as a matter of fact, he went away—to Holland, I believe, but," and his face brightened, "his hair has gone quite white, and he has grown a beard!"

"Humph!" said Alice. "I don't see the point of that. But what is that sack for?"

"That's for the Indemnity, Reparations, and Damages, you know, thousands of millions! I had to get a very big sack to hold it all!"

"But it seems quite empty," Alice said, looking at the loose folds. "Didn't you get the money?"

"Well, not exactly! I didn't actually get it, but I've got the bag ready. You see, it's as well to be prepared for *everything*. If the thousands of millions should happen to come in it would never do not to have something to put the money in."

"It looks to me," said Alice, "like counting your chickens before they were hatched, and not having even the eggs to count by."

The Knight looked vexed, and muttered something about "unforeseen circumstances".

"And what is that big Extinguisher for?" Alice went on to inquire.

"Now, that's an invention I'm rather proud of," said the Knight. "I invented it to extinguish Mr Asquith."

"But did it?" Alice asked.

"Not quite," said the Knight, with a frown. "Not quite—he must have got out somehow. at any rate, he's not there now, but the invention was all right—it wasn't my fault that it didn't work."

"And what is the meaning of that box with the bottom open?" said Alice.

"That's the Treasury Box," said the Knight, proudly. "You see, you put the money in through the slit at the top—"

"And it all tumbles out at the bottom," said Alice. "Don't you see it is wide open?"

"Dear me!" said the Knight, glancing round at the box. "So it is! I must speak to Geddes about it."

"And what is that sieve?" asked Alice.

"Oh! That's our great Economy Invention," said the Knight, eagerly. "It saves such a lot in liquidation, you'd be surprised!"

"Yes," said Alice. "I expect I should be. But what is that doll's house for?"

"That's one of my model homes for heroes! Hundreds of thousands of them are all over the country!"

"But are they all over the country?" Alice asked.

"Well, not quite all over the country," said the Knight, looking a little embarrassed, "not exactly all over the country, but they would be if they had been built."

"But the heroes ca'n't live in them if they're not built, can they?" Alice remarked.

"Ah! But it's something to go by in case they are built, and perhaps some day—"

"I don't think much of your inventions so far," said Alice. "But I see you have some golf-clubs—do you golf?"

"I take them about with me when I go to sea-side Conferences," said the Knight, with a satisfied smile, "so that I can teach the game to Foreign Prime Ministers."

"That is interesting," said Alice. "Do they make good pupils?"

"Well, not exactly," said the Knight. "Now, I dare say you noticed when you first saw me just now that I was looking a little thoughtful."

"You were a little grave," said Alice.

"Well, I was just wondering why it is that the Foreign Prime Ministers are always called home in a hurry when I begin teaching them!"

"Perhaps they don't like your swing," said Alice. "And now, what is that bee-hive for?"

"That's the hive of British Industry where the busy bees, you know, make the honey."

"But there don't seem to be any bees about it; are they all asleep or dead?"

"There aren't many bees about, not just now," the Knight admitted, "but there's a hive all ready for them when they *do* come."

The horse, which had been getting a little restive, began to move on, with the Knight pulling hard at the reins, and Alice noticed that it had spiked anklets round its feet.

"What are they for?" Alice asked. "Protection?"

"No, no, not Protection!" said the Knight, hastily, "not exactly Protection, but simply as a safeguard against Dumping, you know!"

The horse trotted off down the glade, bearing its rider, the various inventions jingling as they went, and disappeared into the wood.

Afterword to the 2010 edition

BY HUGH CAHILL,
KING'S COLLEGE LONDON

Party moves on either side,
Checks and feints that don't deceive
Knights and Bishops, Pawns and all,
In a game of Make-Believe.

Things that fall contrariwise,
Difficult to understand
Darkly through a Looking-Glass
Turvey-wise in Wonderland.

The Westminster Alice is an inspired satire on the political events of the years 1900–1902, a time when the initial enthusiasm of the British public for the Boer War was on the wane and hard questions were being asked about how the government was handling it. First published in the *Westminster Gazette*, it is a perfect blend of word and image, taking the works of Lewis Carroll and the illustrations of Sir John Tenniel as inspiration, and captures perfectly the topsy-turvy nature of the world created by Carroll, transposing it to Westminster.

The Westminster Alice is the result of the collaboration of Hector Hugh Munro (1870–1916), best remembered today for his short-stories, who wrote under the pen-name Saki (a character in the Rubaiyat of Omar Khayyám) and the cartoonist Francis Carruthers Gould (1844–1925). Munro had not long embarked on a career as a writer when mutual friends in Devon introduced him to Gould. Gould was already a celebrated cartoonist and, recognizing the young Munro as a natural talent, took him under his wing. As C. H. Gillen has pointed out, they formed an unlikely partnership; politically Gould was a Liberal and radical in his views while Munro was a Tory and somewhat reactionary in his.[1] Despite these political differences their friendship prospered and early in the summer of 1900 they met with J. A. Spender, the editor of the *Westminster Gazette,* with a proposal for a series of political satires inspired by the works of Lewis Carroll. Spender had misgivings at first, having had numerous such parodies come across his desk, most of which were dismal, but he was impressed by Munro and let the project proceed.

The first piece appeared in July 1900 and the series continued until early 1902. It proved so popular that the parts were collected and reprinted in a pamphlet "with apologies to Sir John Tenniel and to everybody else concerned". As in many of his later stories, as Carolyn Sigler points out, Saki uses a child to reveal social hypocrisy and pokes fun at the complacency and incompetence of the political classes.[2] However, while we can sense anger and indignation in *The*

---

1   Gillen, Charles H. 1969. *H. H. Munro (Saki).* New York: Twayne, pp. 36–37.

2   Carolyn Sigler, ed. 1997. *Alternative Alices: visions and revisions of Lewis Carroll's Alice books: an anthology.* Lexington: University Press of Kentucky, p. 331.

Westminster Alice, it is much less wild and savage than some of his stories could be.

Although *The Westminster Gazette* was Liberal in its inclinations Saki and Gould did not spare that party. In "Alice in Difficulties", divisions in the upper echelons of the Liberal Party are ridiculed mercilessly with Sir Edward Grey and Lord Rosebery depicted as flamingos, one of which Alice is trying to use as a croquet mallet.[3] Political institutions in general are also criticized; in "Alice at St Stephen's" in a piece satirizing elements of parliamentary procedure, William Court Gully, the then speaker of the House of Commons is depicted as a Caterpillar whose attention Alice finds hard to attract.[4] However, the real focus of attention for Gould and Saki was the government of the day, made up of the Conservatives and the Liberal Unionists (which had been in power since 1895), and its handling of the Boer War.

ALICE AND THE BOER WAR

In "Alice in Downing Street", the opinion that Saki and Gould had of the government is clear—inept. Indeed, A. J. Balfour, First Lord of the Treasury, is represented as an "Ineptitude" and is drawn by Gould as something resembling an extinct Great Auk. The Colonial Secretary, Joseph Chamberlain is the Red Queen who wants to paint everything "khaki", and the Prime Minister, Lord Salisbury, is represented as the lethargic Red King, falling asleep while chaos reigns about him.[5]

---

3   See p. 29 above, note 19.
4   See p. 33 above, note 23.
5   See pp. 7–11 above, notes 2–4.

In "Alice Anywhere but Downing-Street", Saki and Gould again target government inaction and failure to fulfil its promises. Alice is being examined by the Red Queen (Joseph Chamberlain) and the White Queen (A. J. Balfour).[6] The first subject is Christian Science with the White Queen asking Alice:

"If there was a sort of warfare going on in a kind of a country, and you wanted to stop it, and didn't know how to, what course of inaction would you pursue?"

"Action you mean. Her White Majesty occasionally muddles things," interposed the Red Queen.

"It amounts to much the same thing with us," said the White Queen. Alice pondered. "I suppose I should resign," she hazarded
Both Queens gasped and held up their hands in reprobation.

"An improper suggestion," said the White Queen severely. "Now I should simply convince my reasoning faculty that the war didn't exist—and there'd be an end of it."

Attention is then turned to the subject of old age pensions. The Salisbury government had long promised to introduce such pensions but had come under criticism from the Opposition for failing to fulfil that promise.[7] We return to our protagonists when they have turned to the subject of Political Economy. The Red Queen asks Alice:

"Supposing you were pledged to introduce a scheme for Old Age Pensions, what would be your next step?"

Alice considered. "I should think—"

"Of course you'd think," said the White Queen, "ever so much. You'd go on thinking on and off for years. I ca'n't tell you how much I've thought about it myself; I still think about it a little, just for practice—principally on Tuesdays."

"I should think," continued Alice, without noticing the interruption, "that the first thing would be to find the money."

6   See p. 25 above, notes 16 and 17.
7   See p. 26 above, note 18.

"Dear, no," said the Red Queen pityingly, " that wouldn't be Political Economy. The first thing would be to find an excuse for dropping the question."

In "Alice has Tea at the Hotel Cecil" Balfour appears as the March Hare, Chamberlain as the Mad Hatter and Lord Salisbury as the Dormouse. Salisbury's government was known as Hotel Cecil because of the number of members of the Cecil family in it.[8] Saki here targets the failure of the government to implement all the things it had promised to do despite being in power since 1895:

> Alice looked at a long list of dishes with promising names, but nearly all of them seemed to be crossed off.
>
> "That list was made nearly seven years ago, you know," said the March Hare, in explanation.
>
> "But you can always have patience," said the Hatter. "You begin with patience and we do the rest." And he leaned back and seemed prepared to do a lot of rest.

However, Saki again returns to the subject of the war and inability of the government to bring it to a conclusion. He has the Hatter sing the following verse:

> *Dwindle, dwindle, little war,*
> *How I wonder more and more,*
> *As about the veldt you hop*
> *When you really mean to stop.*

We are also treated to one of Gould's more amusing pictures with the Hatter and March Hare, trying to force the Dormouse into a martial pose in and effort to make him look more like a "lion" than a mouse and failing miserably.

One of the most successful of the pieces is "Alice in Pall Mall" where Lord Lansdowne, Secretary of State for War

---

8   See p. 44 above, note 30.

between 1895 and 1900, is depicted as the White Knight.[9]
Lansdowne received much of the blame for Britain's
unpreparedness for war and for the setbacks suffered by the
troops in South Africa. However, when the Conservatives and
Liberal Unionists were returned to power in the so-called
"khaki election" of 1900, he was promoted to Foreign
Secretary, a post which Salisbury had filled himself since
1895. Lansdowne is depicted switching horses from one
marked "WO" (War Office) to the other marked "FO"
(Foreign Office).

> "The great art of falling off a horse," said the White Knight, "is to
> have another handy to fall on to."
> "But wouldn't that be rather difficult to arrange?" asked Alice.
> "Difficult, of course," replied the Knight, "but in my Department
> one has to be provided for emergencies. Now have you for instance
> ever conducted a war in South Africa?"
> Alice shook her head.
> "I have," said the Knight, with a gentle complacency in his voice.
> "And did you bring it to a successful conclusion?" asked Alice
> "Not exactly to a conclusion—not a *definite* conclusion, you know—
> nor entirely successful either. In fact I believe it's going on still…"

His perceived incompetence and short-sightedness are
mocked; pointing out the obsolete gun tied to his saddle, he
explains why he equipped the troops with them:

> "Why do you suppose I sent out guns of that particular kind? Because
> if they happened to fall into the hands of the enemy they'd be very
> little use to him. That was my own invention."

Later Saki ridicules Lansdowne for underestimating the
fighting abilities of the Boers:

---

9   See p. 12 above, note 6.

"They appeared in strength at places that weren't even marked on the ordinary maps. But how do you think they got there?"

He paused and fixed his gently eye upon Alice as she walked alongside him, and then continued in a hollow voice, "They rode. Rode and carried rifles. They were no mortal foes—they were Mounted Infantry."

This was perhaps the best received of Gould's and Saki's pieces at the time. J A Spender, editor of the *Westminster Gazette*, wrote in an introduction to a later edition *The Westminster Alice*:

> Of the many political squibs I can remember none had so immediate and complete success as this. It was quoted everywhere, and the whole town joined in the laugh.[10]

It was not only the political leadership that came in for criticism over the prosecution of the war. In "Alice Lunches at Westminster" Gould and Saki turn their attention to the military leadership, and in particular, General Sir Redvers Buller who had been commander-in-chief of the forces in South Africa (1899–1900) before being superseded by Frederick Sleigh Roberts. He is depicted as Humpty Dumpty in military uniform.[11] Buller had returned from the war in South Africa in November 1900 to a rapturous reception and in October 1901 was appointed as commander of the newly formed First Army Corps at Aldershot. This appointment was much criticized in the press, particularly in *The Times*. Much of this criticism was provoked by a message Buller had sent to Lord Lansdowne suggesting that the besieged Ladysmith be surrendered and another to Sir George White, the commander there, that he surrender on the best terms he could negotiate. At a luncheon at Queen's Hall, Westminster, on 10 October 1901 Buller defended his appointment, suggesting that his

10 See p. xiii above.
11 See p. 36 above, note 25.

message to White had been misconstrued and that he had not
instructed him to surrender but had merely wanted to give
him "some sort of cover" if he was obliged to surrender.[12]
Buller's confused speech was unconvincing and did not answer
his critics. The government cancelled Buller's appointment
soon after he made the speech on the grounds that by making
it he had broken regulations. As Carroll had put incompre-
hensible doggerel into Humpty Dumpty's mouth, Saki takes
a swipe at the competence of the British military leadership by
having Buller repeat his confused speech to Alice in nonsense
verse:

> I sent a message to the White
> To tell him—if you MUST, you might;
> But then, I said, you p'raps might
> (The weather was EXTREMELY hot).
>
> This query, too, I spatchcock-slid,
> How would you do it, if you did?
> I did not know, I rather thought—
> And then I wondered if I ought."

ALICE IN WIDER SOCIETY

Politicians were not the only targets for Gould and Saki. In
"Alice goes to Lambeth" their target is the Church of England
and its critics. In Gould's picture we see the then Archbishop
of Canterbury, Frederick Temple ,depicted as the Duchess
with a baby dressed in priestly garb, which "kept wriggling
itself into all manner of postures and uncompromising
attitudes" in her lap. Scattered at the feet of the Duchess are
a smouldering candle and a censer. In the corner is the cook,
looking remarkably like Samuel Smith MP, a strident critic in

12 "Sir R. Buller and his critics", in *The Times*, Friday, 11 October
    1901, p. 10.

Parliament of "ritualism" within the Church of England.[13] He is stirring the "protestant" pot and "pausing every now and then to fling a reredos or half rubric at the Duchess".

During Temple's time as Archbishop of Canterbury there was much controversy about certain Anglican priests using incense and lights in the liturgy, as well as practices such as hearing confession, saying prayers for the dead and the reservation of the sacrament. Temple disliked most of these practices but was reluctant to take action against clergy who used them, believing that if the bishops were firm and simply gave clear guidance on their legality under Church law the clergy would give them up. In 1899 Temple was asked to offer an opinion on the legality of the reservation of the host and the use of lights and incense in services. He held a hearing at Lambeth and after listening to the evidence presented to him he judged that such practices were not permitted.[14] These practices continued, however. Saki has Alice ask the Duchess why she does not exert her authority, to which she replies:

> "My dear, it takes me all the exertion I can spare to have any authority. I give orders, and it's my endeavour not to see that they're disobeyed. I'm sure I've given this child my Opinion—but there, you might as well opine to a limpet. As to the cook—"

At this point the cook throws a pepper pot at the Duchess.

Unlike the political satires we do not sense real anger behind the jibes, only amusement. Saki did not take religion seriously; in the future he would frequently satirize it in his short stories and in his history *The rise of the Russian Empire* (1900) he had treated the subject with amused contempt.[15] This

---

13 See p. 17 above, notes 8 and 9.
14 Hinchliff, Peter. 1998. *Frederick Temple, Archbishop of Canterbury: a life*. Oxford: Clarendon Press, p. 275–280.
15 Gillen, Charles H. 1969. *H. H. Munro (Saki)*. New York: Twayne, pp. 31–32.

amusement is clear from the closing line of the piece. When the baby disappears the Cheshire-Cat appears and asks where it has gone. "It went out—to roam, I think," replied Alice, to which the Cheshire-Cat responds pointedly, "I always said it would."

In "Alice in a Fog" even Alfred Austin, the Poet Laureate, found himself the subject of satire. Indeed, Austin's poetry had been the subject of Gould's satire on previous occasions. In 1901 the Duke of York (the future King George V) and his wife visited Australia to attend the first session of the Australian Commonwealth Parliament on 7 May 1901.[16] Austin wrote an ode to greet them on their return and is depicted as the White Rabbit hurrying to present them with the lines he has written. It is clear that Saki thinks little of Austin's verses:

> "It seems to be a kind of poetry," said Alice doubtfully; "At least," she added, "some of the words rhyme and none of them appear to have any meaning."

The Westminster Alice series had run its course by early 1902 but between February and November of 1902 Gould and Munro collaborated on more political parodies for the *Westminster Gazette*, *The Political Jungle Book* and the *Not So Stories*, which took the works of Rudyard Kipling as their model. Again, Balfour was one of Saki's targets appearing as Sheer Khan't, the tiger. These parodies did not capture the public imagination in the same way the *Alice* series had, however.

In 1901 Saki began publishing witty and satirical stories about a young man named Reginald, which were later published in book form in 1904. The following year he went to the Balkans as a correspondent for the *Morning Post*, later

16 See p. 39 above, note 27.

moving on to Warsaw, St Petersburg and Paris, returning finally to London in 1908. He continued to write short stories which appeared in the *Morning Post* and in other Tory newspapers. These stories were later collected and appeared as *The Chronicles of Clovis* (1911), *Beasts and Super-Beasts* (1914), *The Toys of Peace* (1919), and *The Square Egg* (1924). He also published two novels, *The Unbearable Bassington* (1912) and *When William Came* (1913), a picture of England under the German yoke after having been invaded by the Kaiser's army. At the outbreak of war in 1914 Saki enlisted in the ranks despite his age and refusing a commission. He was killed in action on the 14 November 1916 at the Battle of Ancre. His body was never found.[17]

Gould provided the illustrations for Charles Geake's *John Bull's Adventures in the Fiscal Wonderland* (1904) and when the Liberal party was returned to power in 1906 he was knighted for his political services. He continued to publish cartoons and illustrate books, retiring in 1914. Gould died in 1925 at his home in Porlock in Somerset.[18]

Somewhat surprisingly, given that the events it satirized would have been by that time obscure, *The Westminster Alice* was published in an American edition in 1929. Yet its appeal was such that the publishers were overwhelmed by requests from booksellers and the edition quickly sold out. With an even greater period of time having elapsed between the events related in *The Westminster Alice*, the modern reader might find it hard to appreciate without copious footnotes. However,

---

17 Elton, Godfrey. 1927. "Munro, Hugh Hector (1870-1916)" in *Dictionary of National Biography 1912–1921*. London: Oxford University Press.

18 For further information on Gould's life and career see "Sir F. C. Gould' (Obituary)" in *The Times*, 2 January 1925, p. 12, and Grimsditch, H. B. 1937. "Gould, Sir Francis Carruthers (1844–1925)", in *Dictionary of National Biography 1922–1930*. London: Oxford University Press.

perseverance will be rewarded with a witty insight into the political events of just over a hundred years ago—events with many parallels to our own time.

FURTHER READING

Gillen, Charles H. 1969. *H. H. Munro (Saki)*. New York: Twayne.

Hinchliff, Peter. 1998. *Frederick Temple, Archbishop of Canterbury: a life*. Oxford: Clarendon Press.

Munro, H. H. (Saki). [1930] *The short stories of Saki*. [London]: John Lane.

Munro, H. H. (Saki). 1933. *The novels and plays of Saki (H. H. Munro)*. London: Bodley Head.

Carolyn Sigler, ed. 1997. *Alternative Alices: visions and revisions of Lewis Carroll's Alice books: an anthology*. Lexington: University Press of Kentucky.

Spears, George James. 1963. *The satire of Saki: a study of the satiric Art of Hector H. Munro*. New York: Exposition Press.

Eachtraí Eilíse i dTír na nIontas
Alice in Irish, 2007

Lastall den Scáthán agus a bhFuair Eilís Ann Roimpi
Looking-Glass in Irish, 2009

Alys in Pow an Anethow
Alice in Cornish, 2009

La Aventuroj de Alicio en Mirlando
Alice in Esperanto, 2009

Les Aventures d'Alice au pays des merveilles
Alice in French, 2010

Alice's Abenteuer im Wunderland
Alice in German, 2010

Le Avventure di Alice nel Paese delle Meraviglie
Alice in Italian, 2010

Contoyrtyssyn Ealish ayns Çheer ny Yindyssyn
Alice in Manx, 2010

Alice's Äventyr i Sagolandet
Alice in Swedish, 2010

Anturiaethau Alys yng Ngwlad Hud
Alice in Welsh, 2010

Lightning Source UK Ltd.
Milton Keynes UK
08 August 2010